Waterfalls

Waterfalls

Andrew Donnelly

THE CHILD'S WORLD®, INC.

Library of Congress Cataloging-in-Publication Data
Donnelly, Andrew.
  Waterfalls / by Andrew Donnelly.
      p.   cm.
  Includes index.
  Summary: Questions and answers present
information about the characteristics, causes,
effects, and locations of waterfalls.
  ISBN 1-56766-487-3 (lib. bdg. : acid-free paper)
  1. Waterfalls—Juvenile literature.
[1. Waterfalls—Miscellanea. 2. Questions and answers.] I. Title.
        GB1403.8.D66   1998
      551.48′4—dc21   97-44403
                                CIP
                                AC

Photo Credits

© Beth Davidow: 6, 30
© Comstock, Inc.: 9
© Daniel J. Cox/Natural Exposures: 20
© David N. Davis: 19
EARTH SCENES © Ralph A. Reinhold: 15
© Gary Braasch/Tony Stone Images: 26
© Gene Boaz: 10
© 1996 Greg Gawlowski/Dembinsky Photo Assoc. Inc: 23
© H. Richard Johnston/Tony Stone Worldwide: 13
© Kevin Schafer: 2, 16
© Michael Busselle/Tony Stone Images: cover
© Paul Souders/Tony Stone Images: 24
© Tom Dietrich/Tony Stone Worldwide: 29

On the cover...

Front cover: This beautiful waterfall is trickling over some rocks.
Page 2: This waterfall tumbles down a hill in Costa Rica.

Table of Contents

Welcome to the Waterfall!

As the summer sun blazes in the sky, you watch a lazy river drifting by. Walking alongside, you see the river start to move faster. You hear a low roar, like that of distant thunder. The farther downstream you walk, the faster the water moves and the louder the roar becomes. Finally, you turn a corner and the river seems to disappear! Then you see a crashing, swirling stream of water falling hundreds of feet into a cloud of mist. You have come upon one of nature's most wonderful sights—a waterfall!

← This powerful waterfall is found in Yellowstone National Park.

What Is a Waterfall?

Most of the time, a river moves calmly over nearly flat ground. Sometimes, however, the water falls off a cliff or the side of a mountain. When this happens, the dropping water is called a waterfall. Waterfalls are very noisy. The water makes noise as it splashes down and hits the bottom.

Big waterfalls like this one make a lot of noise. ⇒

Are There Different Types of Waterfalls?

Just as there are different sizes of cliffs, there are different types of waterfalls. The ground under a river is called a **riverbed**. Some riverbeds are rough and filled with rocks. As the water goes over these bumps, it moves very fast and looks like hundreds of tiny waterfalls. These little waterfalls are called **rapids**.

A slightly bigger waterfall, or a series of them, is called a **cascade**. A huge waterfall is called a **cataract**. *Niagara Falls*, which is between the United States and Canada, is a famous cataract.

⇐ Rapids like these carry the water in many different directions.

Where Do Waterfalls Occur?

You can find waterfalls in almost every country. The more hills and rivers a place has, the more likely it is to have waterfalls. Countries like Norway, Venezuela, and Brazil have many waterfalls. In the United States, the states of California, Washington, and Oregon each have over 200 waterfalls!

This small waterfall is hidden deep in a forest. ⇒

Small streams and slow-moving water usually have smaller cascades. Large, powerful cataracts usually occur in larger, fast-moving rivers. In Niagara Falls, 15 million cubic feet of water drop over the cliff every minute. That much water would fill a football field 250 feet deep every minute!

Niagara Falls is a very powerful cataract. ⇒

How High Are Waterfalls?

Niagara Falls is a huge waterfall, but at only 160 feet, it is nowhere near the tallest. The tallest waterfall in the United States is *Yosemite* (yo–SEH–mih–tee) *Falls* in California. This waterfall is over 2,400 feet tall!

For a long time, Yosemite Falls was thought to be one of the tallest in the world. Then, in 1935, a pilot was searching for gold in the hills of Venezuela. As he flew into canyon after canyon, he came upon an incredible sight—a river going straight down! What he found was *Angel Falls*, the world's tallest waterfall. It is over 3,200 feet tall. That is almost three times as tall as the Empire State Building!

⇐ In this picture, Angel Falls is even higher than the clouds.

What Causes Waterfalls?

Waterfalls can form for many different reasons. Most big waterfalls start on hills that have a layer of hard rock over softer ground. The river slowly wears away the soft ground, causing the bottom of the hill to break away. That leaves a cliff of hard rock with a waterfall over the edge.

This little waterfall in Kentucky was formed many years ago. ⇒

Some waterfalls happen when a mountain stream forms a new path over the edge of the mountain. Other waterfalls form when the ground moves in an earthquake. *Sinkholes,* or places where the ground collapses, can cause waterfalls, too.

Do Animals Live by Waterfalls?

As the water falls to the ground, it creates lots of mist in the air. This mist provides plenty of water for plants to grow. Many different types of plants like to grow by waterfalls. With so many plants around, a lot of animals like to live there, too.

This waterfall in Oregon brings water to many different plants. ⇒

As nice as waterfalls are for some animals, they can create problems for fish. Some types of fish need to swim upriver to have their babies. When they meet a waterfall, they are stuck. One type of fish, the *salmon*, has found an interesting way to get past waterfalls or rapids. It jumps over them!

Do People Use Waterfalls?

Waterfalls are very popular. People love to go camping and fishing near them. In fact, waterfalls are so popular that many countries have created parks around them. Some waterfalls are also used as a source of energy. The power of the falling water is turned into electricity. This kind of energy is called **hydroelectric power**. Many countries use electricity made by hydroelectric power. Norway creates 99 percent of its electricity from falling water!

Do Waterfalls Cause Problems?

In the past, waterfalls caused some serious problems. People use boats to move supplies from one place to another. But boats cannot cross waterfalls. Instead, people have learned to build ways around waterfalls. Sometimes they build another water channel, called a **canal**, around the falls. In other cases they build gates that can raise or lower the water level in the river. These gates are called **locks**. Boats can ride up or down in these locks as the water level is changed. Canals and locks are expensive to build, but they are the only way people can travel up and down some rivers.

This lock near Seattle has changed the water level for these boats. ⇒

Are Waterfalls in Danger?

Most waterfalls are either too useful or too big for anyone to destroy. Garbage and chemicals, however, can make the water harmful to animals and plants. Harmful things in the water are called **water pollution**. Many governments, including the United States, now have laws that protect our water.

These laws help, but there is still much we can do. If we visit a waterfall, for example, we can be sure not to leave any trash behind. If we work together, we can keep our waterfalls clean and beautiful for years to come.

⇐ Clean waterfalls like this one in Wyoming are very beautiful.

Glossary

canal (cuh-NAL)
A canal is a waterway built by people. People sometimes build canals so their boats can travel around waterfalls.

cascade (kas–KADE)
A cascade is a medium-sized waterfall or a series of small waterfalls. Many rivers and streams have cascades.

cataract (KAT-uh-rakt)
A cataract is a very large waterfall. Niagara Falls is a cataract.

hydroelectric power (hy-droh-ee–LEK–trik POW–er)
Hydroelectric power is electricity made from the energy of moving water. Waterfalls can produce a great deal of energy.

locks (LOKS)
Locks are gates that raise and lower the water level along sections of a river. Boats can ride up and down in the locks to move past waterfalls.

rapids (RA–pidz)
Rapids are fast-moving, rough waters that look like hundreds of little waterfalls. Rapids occur when a river flows over lots of rocks.

riverbed (RIH–ver–bed)
A riverbed is the ground under a river. Certain kinds of riverbeds are more likely to have waterfalls.

water pollution (WAH–ter puh–LOO–shun)
Water pollution occurs when garbage and chemicals make the water dirty. Some waterfalls have polluted water.

Index